Night

By Pauline Cartwright

I can hear the tree outside my window.
Rustle, rustle, rustle.
I hear it every night.

Rustle, rustle, rustle.

I can hear the clock on the wall.
Tick, tick, tick.
I hear it every night.

4

Tick, tick, tick.

I can hear the cats fighting.
Yowl, yowl, yowl.
I hear them every night.

Yowl, yowl, yowl.

I can hear Grandad sleeping.
Snore, snore, snore.
I hear him every night.

Snore, snore, snore.

9

I can hear Mom and Dad.
Talk, talk, talk.
I hear them every night.

Talk, talk, talk.

I can hear noises in the hall.
Sniff, sniff, pitter-patter.
What is out there?

"Toby!
Come in, Toby!
Shhh. Mom and Dad will hear."

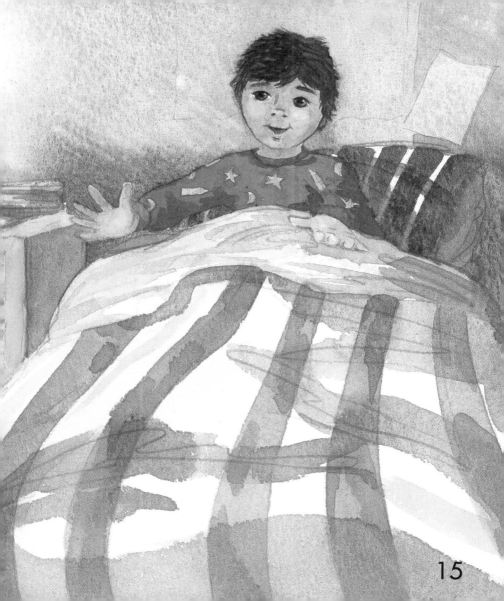

"We can hear the night noises together."